The Barbarians

Special Edition
Created by Angel Entertainment Inc.

Published in the U.S. by
Marboro Books, a division of
Barnes and Noble Bookstores, Inc.

YOUNG DISCOVERY LIBRARY

Library of Congress Cataloging-in-Publication Data

Bombarde, Odile.
  [Long voyage des Barbares. English]
  The Barbarians/author, Odile Bombarde; illus., Donald Grant.
  Translation of: Le long voyage des Barbares.
  Includes index.
  1. Migrations of nations — Juvenile literature. 2. Rome —
History — Germanic Invasions, 3d-6th centuries — Juvenile
literature. I. Grant, Donald. II. Title. III. Series: Young Discovery
Library; (Series): 10.   87-34092
D135.B6613   1988   937 — dc19   ISBN 0-944589-10-3
Printed and bound by L.E.G.O., Vicenza, Italy

Written by Odile Bombarde
Illustrated by Donald Grant

Specialist adviser:
Dominique Barthélemy,
Master Lecturer
University of Paris

ISBN 0-944589-10-3
First U.S. Publication 1988 by
Young Discovery Library
217 Main St. • Ossining, NY 10562

©Editions Gallimard, 1987
Translated by Ann M. TenEyck
English text © by Young Discovery Library.
Thanks to Irene Coleman Dillon

YOUNG DISCOVERY LIBRARY

Who invented the word "barbarian"?

The Greeks did, as long ago as the 5th century, B.C. This word designated all those who did not speak as they did. "Bar-bar" imitates the sound of a strange language which sounds like muttering when one does not understand it. Bit by bit, proud of their civilization, the Greeks treated their barbaric foes with contempt, especially the Persians of Asia who tried to invade them. Living freely in the city, the Greeks thought the Barbarians, who obeyed a king, were slaves who loved only riches and fought in a disorderly manner. Their customs seemed eccentric because they were different.

◀ On the plain of Marathon, a small number of Athenian soldiers pushed back the armies of the King of Persia.

In Athens, the Acropolis is dedicated to the goddess of reason, Athena.

An invasion begins:
one winter's night, 15,000 Germanic
Barbarians crossed the frozen Rhine river.

Rome built an immense empire with its conquests. But Rome declined. **The Barbarian peoples arrived!** Fleeing their countries of steppes and forests where they did not have the means to live, they looked towards the rich, civilized regions of the south and east. At first, Rome made them soldiers and allies. Then their migrations became invasions of pillaging warriors. Between Ancient Times and the Middle Ages, the Barbarians brought chaos to Europe and North Africa, but they also brought a new vitality into the divided Roman world.

The emperors erected columns on which were carved the stories of their victories over the Barbarians.

As long as the Romans were powerful, they were able to defend against Barbarian attacks.

Soon the Visigoths were in Spain, the Vandals in Africa, the Ostrogoths in Italy, the Franks in the north of Gaul and Germany, the Saxons in England.

IRELAND

ENGLAND

Jutes

Angles

Saxons

GERMANY

Franks

Burgundians

GAUL
(France)

Visigoths

Rome

SPAIN

Vandals

AFRICA

Vandals

Lombards

Huns

Ostrogoths

Visigoths

The eastern Roman Empire in Byzantium lasted for more than 1,000 years.

ITALY

GREECE

11

Daring Warriors

The Barbarians destroyed human lives, roads, monuments, businesses and farms. They wanted neither to create nor to produce. Their greatest honor was to die in combat.

Barbarian boys were trained to become hunters and warriors.

As soon as they were of age, they carried arms: a lance, a long sword later adopted by the knights of the Middle Ages, and an ax which they threw at the enemy.

Stilicho, a Vandal who became a Roman general, fought against the Visigoths.

The Barbarians frightened the Romans because they were big, strong and courageous...

... and they had startling habits, like buttering their hair.

The Huns came from Asia.

These nomadic warriors drove other Barbarians ahead of them. They inspired terror because of their ferocity, their deadly bows and the scars on their faces. They had no written language but their artwork was fascinating.

They lived on horseback, hunted and raised cattle.

It is said that they ate raw meat which was served to them in the saddle!

Their cities were camps with wooden palaces, tents and chariots.

Attila, their king, was a skilled politician who founded a large kingdom in Hungary before attacking Gaul and then Italy. But he was beaten by the Romans. After him the empire of the Huns collapsed.

The Bishop of Tours brought gold to Attila so he would spare the city.

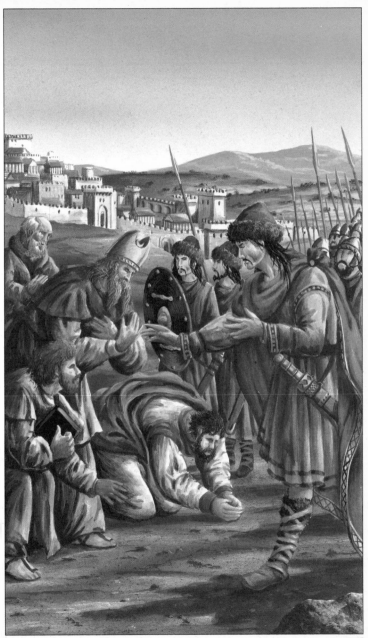

Have you ever heard the word "vandal" used to describe someone who enjoys destroying things?
The Vandals were a savage people. They ravaged Spain, then within ten years, seized North Africa and took the Roman cities there, with their rich storehouses of wheat. They abused the people. From that time, the name Vandals represented the enemies of civilization, science and the arts!

Next they built a fleet of fast boats and became pirates on the Mediterranean Sea.
Then, led by their chief, Genseric, they disembarked in Italy, burning and pillaging Rome and its superb monuments for fifteen days.
Several years later the last Roman emperor fled. He was a child named Romulus, like the founder of Rome.

The Franks, whose name means "the proud ones," were among the first Barbarians to form a permanent kingdom. Their leader, Clovis, was a soldier who was brutal, ignorant and a real bandit. King at 15 years old, he built a powerful army with which he won many victories. He annexed several peoples and established his troops on a territory which stretched from the Rhine river to the Atlantic Ocean. His wife, Clotilda, urged him to become a Christian. After his baptism, the Gallo-Roman bishops helped him. He succeeded in uniting his people with the local Christians.

Childeric, father of Clovis, carried by his warriors.

The Vase of Soissons, which Clovis wanted very much, was broken by a warrior. A year later, Clovis killed the warrior in revenge.

St. Remi, Bishop of Reims, baptized Clovis in a dazzling ceremony.

The Barbarians were only a small part of the population in Europe and they were not the only danger to the people. The **plague,** a spreading disease, took many victims.

The inhabitants of the towns left for the countryside where it was easier for them to find food. Villages were established. Land was going to become the basis of wealth. The Barbarians put fences around the fields they cultivated. They raised goats and sheep. The richer ones hunted wild boar, stag and wild oxen in the forests where they also found wolves and wildcats.

Wood, easier to handle, replaced stone in construction.

Trade was reduced. Luxury goods came from the East.

The Barbarian kings minted their own money, like the Romans. Not much used, it was mainly for prestige.

The Barbarians settled in the countryside. Their servants, when they had them, cultivated the fields.

They used the Roman roads less — river travel and trading became more common.

The Barbarians raised animals on their new holdings. Slaves worked as blacksmiths, shepherds, weavers...

The Barbarians liked flashy jewelry, bright colors, precious stones and weapons. They were very skillful working on leather, wood and metal. The dead were buried with their riches. Gold brooches, swords garnished with silver, sumptuous crowns and decorated shields were found in their tombs. These men knew nature well and honored wild animals like the wolf, bear and eagle. Even after they became Christians, they continued to illustrate them in a simplified way on their ornaments.

Barbarian artisans perfected jewelry making techniques. This one just finished a *cloisonne,* (enameled) gold cross, and an etched belt buckle.

When a king died, his sons divided the kingdom. Sometimes that was very bad. The descendents killed each other. Girls did not count in the succession. A Barbarian king had to maintain peace between his warriors by his decisions. Then he had to reunite them each Spring in order to lead them on raids of other kingdoms!

A new society

Once established among the conquered peoples, the Barbarian customs merged with those remaining from the ancient civilizations, creating a new civilization. They began to speak **Latin,** but added their own words to that language. For example, words such as *pike, bench* and *garden* are all words from early German.

The church was a refuge. Anyone who knocked on its door was under God's protection. In theory, no one was allowed to pursue him there. It was the right of sanctuary.

Sometimes the judges relied on an **ordeal** to indicate God's judgement. If the accused survived a terrible test without injury, such as walking on hot coals, it meant he was innocent.

Some were already Christians and others converted gradually. The Irish monks came to preach to the barbaric peoples.

Each people had its own laws:
To treat one's enemy without mercy was a serious offense. For each offense there was a punishment price. Stealing a dog from a Frank meant paying the price of a grapevine. The murder of a man cost thirty times that; less costly if the victim was a Roman or a woman, especially if she was no longer able to have children.

St. Benedict wrote a Rule of behavior for convents.

When a king died, his sons divided the kingdom. Sometimes that was very bad. The descendents killed each other. Girls did not count in the succession. A Barbarian king had to maintain peace between his warriors by his decisions. Then he had to reunite them each Spring in order to lead them on raids of other kingdoms!

The early French kings had long hair.
It was the mark of royalty. They
moved from place to place with their
nobles, companions, and other members
of their court. They were content to
stay in one place till they had
exhausted its resources, then they
moved their capital to another place.

Mohammed was the founder of a new religion, Islam, whose god is Allah. After Mohammed's death, his followers successfully conquered non-muslim countries.

Three centuries after the first invasion, it was no longer possible to distinguish a Barbarian from the descendent of a Roman citizen!

A new world was in place.

Then the new raiders arrived: the Muslims!

They had already conquered a vast empire, from India to Africa. They defeated the Visigoths in Spain and moved north into Gaul. The Christians united under the leader – ship of Charles Martel, mayor of the capital city of the Franks. He stopped the advancing Muslims near Tours, raided the land south of Gaul and established his power.

The Muslims stayed in Spain for seven hundred years. The beauty of their civilization can be clearly seen in their architecture.

◀ The Legend of Charlemagne...

...and the true face of Charlemagne: he did not have a beard!

Charlemagne was the grandson of Charles Martel. He conquered
a large part of Europe. In the year 800, the pope crowned him emperor. He wanted to govern his empire well and to unite all his people in the Christian faith. At Aix-la-Chapelle, his capital, he built a superb palace and church. He never knew how to write, but spoke several languages, including Latin.

Charlemagne wanted his companions and subjects to be educated. He sent for the monk Alcuin from England, who established the program of the palace school.

**The Vikings arrived from the
North to attack Europe.**
England and Ireland were the first
to suffer their raids. People
prayed in the churches: "Lord,
protect us from the Viking fury!"
The Vikings too, after terrorizing
the people they invaded, were
merged with the conquered people.

Some dates in the history of the Barbarians.

Fifth century, B.C., war of the
    Greeks against the Persians.

Third century, A.D., first invasions
    of the Barbarians.

406: Germanic Barbarians enter
     Roman Gaul.

409: The Vandals arrive in Spain.

410: The Visigoths take Rome.

429: The Vandals conquer North
     Africa.

450: The Saxons invade
     England.

451: Attila, leader of the Huns is
stopped in Gaul.
455: The Vandals destroy Rome.
Beginning of the Middle Ages.
496: Clovis becomes king of the
Franks.
732: Charles Martel stops the
Muslims.
800: Charlemagne, king of the Franks
and of the Lombards,
becomes emperor.
800-1000: the Vikings ravage the
coasts of Europe. Around 1000
they reached America.
1453: end of the Middle Ages.

Egil's Saga is one of the major medieval Icelandic Sagas. It is a historical narrative that tells the story of a great Viking warrior-poet called Egil Skallagrimsson.

Attack on Hedeby describes what happened when the Vikings attacked a town; in this case, during the raid by Harald Hardrade in 1049.

The Viking

My mother once told me
She'd buy me a longship,
A handsome-oared vessel
To go sailing with Vikings:
To stand at the stern-post
And steer a fine warship,
Then head back for harbor
and hew down some foemen.

(Egil's Saga, Ch. 40)

Attack on Hedeby

From end to end
Hedeby we burned
A mighty deed we did
This surely all must grant.
To Sven we gave good cause
To grieve. By night near dawn
I saw the town in flames,
High from the houses raging.

Index

Books of Discovery for children five through ten...

Young Discovery Library is an international undertaking — the series is now published in nine countries. It is the world's first pocket encyclopedia for children, 120 titles will be published.

Each title in the series is an education on the subject covered: a collaboration among the author, the illustrator, an advisory group of elementary school teachers and an academic specialist on the subject.

The goal is to respond to the endless curiousity of children, to fascinate and educate.

TITLES IN THIS SERIES:

The Barbarians

Odile Bombarde

Here's a complete introduction to the tribes that came to conquer and stayed to settle Europe in the Middle Ages—featuring pictures and descriptions of Attila, the Vikings, Charlemagne and more.

Crocodiles and Alligators

Marie Farré

The daily lives, evolution, eggs, babies and other natural history of the big reptiles from the time they were worshiped in ancient Egypt to today—plus a poem by Lewis Carroll.

Monkeys, Apes and Other Primates

André Lucas

Entertainment and education both abound—as these realistic renderings show dozens of species and engaging text tells why lemurs stay up all night, gorillas are strong, gibbons fly—and more!

Going West: Cowboys and Pioneers

Martine Courtault

Adventures of the pioneers, including details of a two-month trip across the Great Plains, life during the Gold Rush, settling a new town, the Pony Express and everyday life in the old west.

Bears, Big and Little

Pierre Pferrer

Are bears as clumsy as they seem, what do grizzlies eat, how do mother bears raise their young? This book answers these and other important questions as it describes all eight species of bears and their habitats.

Long Ago in a Castle

Marie Farré

Realistic rendering of many castles across Europe open this book-full of facts about castle communities of the Middle Ages—replete with information on building techniques, home life, knights, feasts and lords.

Following Indian Trails

Nicholas Grenier

Information to defy stereotypes and teach how Native Americans came to this land, acquired horses, built villages, taught children about life and protected their land.

Undersea Giants

Patrick Geistdoerfer

Poetry, lore, authoritative renderings and text join in this introduction to whales, seals, dolphins and other sea mammals—with many fascinating facts about communication, reproduction and protection of the species.